Warrior Grandma
The Story of Patricia Locke

Warrior Grandma
The Story of Patricia Locke

by Dr. Littlebrave Beaston
illustrated by Luthando Mazibuko

BELLWOOD
PRESS®

WILMETTE, ILLINOIS

Bellwood Press, Wilmette, Illinois
401 Greenleaf Avenue, Wilmette, Illinois 60091

25 24 23 22   4 3 2 1

Library of Congress Cataloging-in-Publication Data

Names: Beaston, Littlebrave, author. | Mazibuko, Luthando, illustrator.
Title: Warrior grandma : the story of Patricia Locke / by Dr. Little-
  brave Beaston ; illustrations by Luthando Mazibuko.
Other titles: Story of Patricia Locke
Description: Wilmette, Illinois : Bellwood Press, 2022. | Series:
  Change maker | Includes bibliographical references. | Audience:
  Ages 10–12 |
Audience: Grades 4–6
Identifiers: LCCN 2022012429 (print) | LCCN 2022012430 (ebook)
  | ISBN 9781618512130 (trade paperback) | ISBN 9781618512147
  (epub)
Subjects: LCSH: Locke, Patricia, 1928–2001. | Lakota Indians—Bi-
  ography. | Indian women—United States—Biography—Juvenile
  literature. | Women social reformers—United States—Biography—
  Juvenile literature. | Women political activists—United States—Bi-
  ography—Juvenile literature. | Bahai women—United States—Biog-
  raphy—Juvenile literature.
Classification: LCC E99.T34 B43 2022 (print) | LCC E99.T34 (eb-
  ook) | DDC 303.48/4092 [B]—dc23/eng/20220323
LC record available at https://lccn.loc.gov/2022012429
LC ebook record available at https://lccn.loc.gov/2022012430

Cover and book design by Patrick Falso
Illustrations by Luthando Mazibuko

This book is dedicated to Patricia's grandchildren, great-grandchildren, and all grandchildren everywhere, so that you may understand the truth like she did. She is everyone's Uŋčí.

Contents

Acknowledgments

When I first met Patricia, I knew she was special. I noticed her friendly smile and could sense her warm spirit. Even though we had never met before, her sparkling eyes, full of wisdom, seemed to say, "I respect and love you." I watched as she greeted everyone in the room in the same manner, and I could tell that she genuinely loved people.

Some people seem to be born with a list of goals they wish to accomplish, and Patricia was one of those people. She had a keen sense of justice, and whenever she was confronted with injustice, she would act to remedy the situation. She was a no-nonsense kind of person.

Writing this book brought back memories of when I lived at Standing Rock, which lies between what is now North and South Dakota. In my mind, I hear the cattle bellowing from a distant ranch and see the horses gathering at a nearby bridge. I recall the tribe's buffalo grazing on the grass as they move from corner to corner in their fenced area. I see myself on the pow-wow grounds, where the Master of Ceremonies (MC) wants to begin the dancing. He calls out, "Hókahe!"(hoke-a-hey). In English, it means, "Let's go."

These are wonderful memories, and I know that Patricia experienced these events as well. I want to thank the Locke family for giving me insights into Patricia's life. Several members of the family and I have been friends for a long time. My gratitude and appreciation go to Gloria Geiser and Christopher Martin for their editing acumen; Karen Jentz and Debra Noble, who served as readers and offered suggestions; and to Nat Yogachandra and Bahhaj Taherzadeh for giving me the opportunity to write this story. I am honored to have the love and support of my son, Damen Gilland. And finally, a belly rub and a treat go to my grand girls—Ellie, the red Australian cattle dog, and Maggie, the pit bull mix—for helping me keep my spiritual balance, with their hugs and kisses, throughout the writing process.

With humility and enthusiasm, I have written this account of Patricia's life. I learned so much from her. She was a true "Change Maker."

Introduction

This is the story of Patricia Locke, who for much of her life was an advocate for Indigenous people's tribal rights. An *advocate* is someone who speaks directly to political leaders in an attempt to pass new laws or to make existing laws more just for everyone. Patricia fought for Indigenous people to have the same rights as everyone else in the United States.

Standing up for and speaking out on behalf of others were in Patricia's genes. When she was still a child, she presented a demonstration in dance and storytelling with her parents in Fort Hall, Idaho, and the experience never left her. She was proud of her heritage, and she learned from her mother and grandfather how to advocate on behalf of others. Her grandfather advocated on behalf of their tribe against the US government to ensure that its treaties with Indians were honored in the late 1800s.[1]

Early in her life, Patricia learned a dirty little secret that was in plain sight for anyone who cared to look. The US Constitution implied that everyone was equal, but Patricia gradually realized that Indians were being treated differently from other people and that her culture was not being given the same respect as that of white Americans. In fact, the Indian way of life was being trampled on in many ways. For example, Indigenous people were being shut out of opportunities in education, and they often did not have the best schooling experiences. When they went to schools available to them, they were taught how to do menial tasks rather than the subjects that would give them a solid foundation for pursuing a higher education. Instead, the education they received focused on teaching them to be "white" rather than who they were—Indigenous. Sometimes they were not allowed to attend "white" schools.

Many Indigenous people experienced this hostility and prejudice all the way through college. In 1940, only six colleges were open to Indigenous people, and one of them was the University of California in Los Angeles, which Patricia attended. The environment was so hostile at times that Patricia would pretend to be Hawaiian if she knew that those in charge would not let her attend an event, such as a meeting of some sort. Of course, lying is never a good idea, but she was determined to have the same equal access to campus events as her classmates. This was one way she stood up and fought for herself.

During this time of her life, Patricia was disappointed to realize that the principles in the Constitution were not being applied to Indigenous people. After all, they had been living on the North American continent—which, according to Iroquois creation stories, was called "Turtle Island"—long before anyone else. She decided she would work with lawmakers to fight for equality for Indians.

When Patricia set out to advocate for Indigenous people, sometimes other people would oppose her work and would try to silence her, but she often used her critical thinking and excellent research skills to throw her opponents off guard. They never took as much time as she did to prepare. She was a good writer, and she had the four Ps—purpose, planning, patience, and persistence. While she had a charming personality and preferred gentleness, humor, and cooperation, her resolve could come across as intimidating for some people. Many politicians, even though they may have disagreed with her, were very impressed by her passion for the cause of equality for Indigenous people.

With steadfastness and determination, she entered the political realm to make life better for the American Indian. She reminded the US government of its treaties with Indigenous people and the need for those treaties to be honored. She spoke up for the right of Indian tribes to govern themselves, to make their own decisions, and to determine their own futures. Justice was her main mantra, and she was willing to fight for it at the local, national, and international levels.

Through a twist of life, Patricia learned about the Bahá'í Faith. A few years later, she fully embraced it and became a Bahá'í. In doing so, she learned a new way to communicate called *consultation*.

How was consultation different than the way she had worked with people before becoming Bahá'í? Was she as effective an advocate for equality? What did she learn that made her embrace the Bahá'í Faith? How did Patricia's upbringing prepare her for such roles?

Let's find out!

1 / Born to Protect

At an early age, Patricia began what was to be her life's work. It started in little steps when she received her first taste of prejudice toward Indians. When the family moved to the Colorado River Tribes Reservation near Parker, Arizona, her mother, Eva, gave Patricia and her little sister, Frances—who was nearly three years younger—some money to go to the movies. They went to the theater and were told that Indians had to sit in the back. Since they were children, they were not tall enough to see over the heads of the other moviegoers.

When Patricia and Frances returned home, Eva asked the girls how the movie was, and they told her they were not able to see it and why. Eva was so furious that she immediately went to the theater and demanded to speak to the owner. She told the owner that she expected him to let her daughters sit wherever they wanted. If he didn't, she said she would have the Indians around the area boycott his theater.

After their mother confronted the owner, Patricia and Frances were allowed to sit wherever they wanted. Patricia never forgot this lesson in speaking out. In fact, you might say it was her first lesson in learning the value of speaking out against injustice, which she would become very skilled at as she grew older.[2]

Patricia was born in Pocatello, Idaho on January 21, 1928. Her parents worked for the Bureau of Indian Affairs (BIA). Her father, John, worked as a clerk, and Eva was a registered nurse and worked in the Indian Health Service.[3] The family moved around frequently and were often placed in BIA housing. They had a big Saint Bernard dog named Patty, which Patricia loved.[4]

Whenever the family moved to a new location, Patricia would always watch out for Frances and make sure no harm came to her. Patricia could be bossy at times, but it came from a place of love.

John and Eva followed traditional Lakota values, which meant they considered a child to be a sacred being, or *Wakȟáŋheža.*[5] They made sure that any caregiver would love and care for Patricia and Frances just as they themselves would.

When Patricia and Frances were too young to go to school, their parents selected a Shoshone medicine man named Tagwits to care for them while they were at work. He was a clever man, and when the girls were cranky, he would begin singing a song and tapping on the table. A broom would then begin to dance to the rhythm of the music. Then the girls would calm down, with smiles on their faces, and the broom would go back to the corner. If you know any medicine people, you know they can do amazing things. Tagwits helped Patricia learn that anything—even something that seemed impossible—could be possible.[6]

Patricia's parents wanted to give their daughters the best education they could. They had many books in their home, as well as magazines such as *The New Yorker*. John and Eva encouraged the girls to read about all sorts of topics. They also gave the girls money for getting good grades as a fun way to instill the importance of doing well in school.[7]

Eva was both Lakota and Dakota, and she knew quite a bit about traditional Lakota ways. John, on the other hand, came from the Mississippi band of the Chippewa, also known as the Ojibwa. While the Ojibwa belong to a group of tribes—called the Anishinaabe—who share cultural similarities, the words *Ojibwa* and *Anishinaabe* are used interchangeably by many Ojibwa. John knew about his own tribe's traditional ways but not those of the Lakota or Dakota. He and Eva were therefore *syncretistic*—that is, they combined different belief systems in their family. They were happy to live with shared beliefs, and many other families also live this way.

John and Eva also attended Catholic Mass with Patricia and Frances so that their daughters could learn more about how to function in both the Indian and the white world. The family felt at ease attending church because the Lakota believe that humanity is one family. The Lakota say, "Mitákuye Oyá'siŋ," and this phrase, loosely translated, means "my relatives everyone." Some people even translate it as "All my Relations." In fact, the Lakota consider humans, animals, sea creatures, plants, and elements such as water and wind to be one family and to be interconnected. The Lakotas constantly strive to achieve *Wólakȟota,* which is translated as *peace* and means to live in balance and harmony with all living creatures.[8]

Eva's father, Noel, stayed with the family occasionally. His Dakota Indian name was *Makȟókiŋyaŋ,* which translated roughly means *Flying Over the Earth.* Patricia and Frances loved their grandfather, and he told them many stories to teach them more of their Dakota values. Indigenous people use stories to make learning fun, and the stories were exciting and taught Patricia and Frances about strength of character and bravery, or *wóochitika.* Some of the stories taught them respect, or *ohóla,* which means *to address a relative.* This value refers to treating everyone with kindness and in a way that honors interconnectedness. Treating everything respectfully shows you have respect for yourself.

Other stories taught the girls generosity, or *wówačhaŋtognaka.* This word refers to the giving of your food, time, experience, and material possessions to those who need them. To give a visitor the best food or to give up your bed for the night is demonstrating generosity. Most stories also taught the virtue of wisdom, or *wóksape*. Wisdom referred to living according to spiritual values and the natural pattern of life.[9]

The girls would sit, spellbound, as they heard the stories of their grandfather. They could listen to these stories all day long.

Along with her book learning, Patricia learned Hoop Dancing, gymnastics, interpretive dance, and some ballet. She also learned how to play tennis and swim. Later in her life, she would teach others these skills to support herself during challenging times.

While they were living in Arizona, Patricia and Frances attended a residential boarding school in the town where their parents were working. At the time, this was the only school in town. And the girls were most likely day students, which meant that, like most kids whose parents worked in the BIA, they went home after school. Patricia was nearly eight, and Frances was five. The nuns who were in charge of the school were very strict, and in addition to classes, students were assigned chores. Patricia helped Frances do her chores, as there were too many for someone of her age. This experience gave

Patricia a glimpse of what it was like for other Indigenous people who went to residential boarding schools, and she was glad to have her mom and dad to go home to.[10]

Eva had taught Patricia to memorize the family home address so she could get help getting home if she ever got lost. This lesson in safety shaped how Patricia would do things all her life. She always thought of ways to solve problems.

One time when Patricia was six years old, Eva took her to Chicago to enter a competition in interpretive dance. She didn't place in the competition, but she had a chance to practice problem solving. Being an inquisitive child, she was exploring her new surroundings when she wandered off and got lost. In a large city such as Chicago, even an adult would have found getting lost daunting and frightening, let alone a child. Where would you start to find your way back?

Patricia kept her cool and found a taxi driver. She was able to give him the name of the hotel she was staying at, and she even thought to tell him that her mother would pay him if he could get her there. Boy, was she thankful to her mother for teaching her to always take note of where she was. Her mother was worried sick but so happy when she arrived. The story could have had a scary ending.

Because the family moved frequently due to John and Eva's jobs, Patricia and Frances had a difficult time maintaining school friends, and they were grateful to have each other. The family moved to Parker, Arizona, and remained there for about two and a half years, and this is where Patricia and Frances had the experience in the movie theater.

They then moved again to the Klamath Agency, which is thirty miles north of Klamath Falls, Oregon, for three years. Patricia challenged herself and read every book in the school library, beginning with titles that began with the letter A all the way through Z. She was fast becoming an avid reader.[11]

During these school years, Patricia had many unusual extracurricular activities. When she was nine years old, she learned American Indian Sign Language from a Nez Percé woman, and she also learned how to sign the 23rd Psalm.[12] At about the same time, her father wanted her to learn classical guitar, so he paid for ten lessons. With only these few lessons, she was able to teach guitar confidently. This was one way in which she was able to help supplement the family income.[13]

The family spent their vacations visiting the Standing Rock Reservation in North and South Dakota, where Eva grew up, and the White Earth reservation in Minnesota, where John had lived as a child. They would also travel to Canada to visit John's relatives. The girls loved these trips. They would listen to stories told by the elders, ride horses, swim in the river, pick chokecherries, make frybread, enjoy the drumming and singing, and of course play with the dogs, which were everywhere.[14]

Patricia and Frances also attended cultural activities, such as powwows, which were held for people to socialize with each other. The girls also learned about the sun dance, or *wiwáŋyaŋg wačhípi,* which was also called the festival of prayer. It was one of the seven rituals taught to the Lakota by the White Buffalo Calf Woman. The participants gaze into the sun as they dance, and the ceremony is dedicated to purification and hope for world peace and unity. Now that it is legal in the United States, the sun dance is held often. It was Patricia's favorite ceremony.

Patricia graduated from high school in Alhambra, California, where her family moved after her father retired. While still a high school student, she tried to figure out where the pope received his authority. This was a perfectly legitimate question, for as a Lakota following her tribal values, she knew the authority for the Sacred Pipe came to the Lakota from the White Buffalo Calf Woman, whom the Lakota revere as a Messenger of God. Some Bahá'ís acknowledge and revere the White Buffalo Calf Woman as well.

However, when she asked the nuns and priests in the area this question, they asked her to accept the pope's authority on faith.

This answer was not good enough for Patricia. She wanted to know the real answer, if there was one.

Eventually, she was referred to the bishop in another town, and she saved up her own money to travel there to see him. When she was able to sit down and talk to the bishop, he turned her away and told her that if she continued asking her question, she would be excommunicated.

Not receiving an answer to her simple question was a disappointment for Patricia. She did not pay much attention to the Church after this experience.[15]

2 / College, Heritage, and Career

In the late 1940s, Patricia attended the John Muir College in Pasadena and later transferred to the University of California in Los Angeles (UCLA). She was the only American Indian enrolled there. Nationwide, there were only six American Indians enrolled in college. This is amazing and hard to imagine, but it is true.[16]

She earned her way through college by teaching swimming lessons at the local YMCA. She even became a member of the women's aquatic ballet team and practiced what today we call "synchronized swimming." Patricia had only two sets of clothes in college. Try living with only two sets of clothes for a week. That would be hard![17]

College was a struggle for her, and her grades suffered to the point that she was placed on probation. *Probation* is a warning that you need to improve your grades, or else you will be expelled from

the school you are attending. She was even suspended from school for a short while. *Suspended* means you can't attend the school for a period of time. However, when she returned to school, she earned better grades and finally graduated in 1951

with a teaching certificate and a Bachelor of Arts. It was an interdepartmental degree in English, anthropology, geology, and physical education.[18]

Patricia later went back to UCLA to pursue a master's degree in public administration, though it's unclear if she was able to complete it due to moving. She always persisted![19]

Patricia taught in a public elementary school for a year but didn't find it rewarding. The curriculum was set up for rote memorization—feeding information to the student without acknowledging the student's own thinking process. She would like to have seen some Lakota values—such as generosity, courage, respect, or a true quest for knowledge—included in the curriculum she was teaching. She also noticed that family ancestry—that is, who descended from whom—was not covered.[20]

Heritage is very important to Lakota people. They know who their relatives are, and some can tell you the names of every single one of their relatives and how they are related. When an Indian meets another from the same tribe, they often ask, "To whom are you related?" or "Who are your parents"? or "Who are your relatives?"

In Patricia's case, she knew the tribes of her parents, and she knew all about her parents' families. For example, she knew that her mother's family were ranchers and that Eva loved horses. She knew that her father had tried to enlist in the military when he was younger. However, since Indians were not US citizens at that time, his application was rejected. Indians couldn't even be drafted for the same reason, so John appealed to a military tribunal, and he was then allowed to enlist. His courage to stand up for his rights opened the doors for himself and for others to serve in World War I.[21]

Patricia knew most of her relatives—even though she had not spent time around all of them—through stories that were told to her by her grandparents and parents. One such story was about her maternal grandfather, whose name was Chief Little Crow. He was a brave man. As chief of the Bdewákhaŋthuŋwaŋ (Mdewankton) Dakota band in the southwest corner of Minnesota, from 1858 to 1862, he sacrificed his time, money, and energy to help his people by traveling to Washington, DC, to ensure that the US government honored the treaties it had made with the Dakota. Unfortunately, the government continually broke these treaties, and his people suffered to the point of starving.[22]

Little Crow worked hard for peace and did not want to take up arms against the

US government unless he absolutely had to. After a while, however, he and his men, in the tradition of the *akíčhita* (warrior), decided they had to resort to using force because they were being cheated out of the government's promised money for food. Fortunately, leaders on both sides decided to meet to see if violence could be avoided. However, in a familiar pattern, due to the prejudicial attitudes of some of the US commanders, the meeting ended poorly.

In 1862, during the Minnesota uprising, both Indians and settlers were killed. Little Crow was shot and killed while picking berries in July of 1863. Then, the day after Christmas in 1863, President

Abraham Lincoln ordered the execution of thirty-eight Dakota Indians in Minnesota. This was totally unjust, as the Indians had been standing up for their rights, fighting for the survival of their families, and expecting the US government to honor its treaties. From then on, many Dakota Indians fled to Canada or other parts of Lakota territory.[23]

Patricia was undoubtedly proud to know that her father and grandfather had stood up for the rights of Indigenous people. Now she is carrying on their legacy in a new way.

Everyone's heritage has certain unique features that make it special and something to be proud of, and you will benefit from knowing as much as possible about your family.

3 / Marriage and Family

Patricia met her future husband, Charles "Ned" Locke, who was of European descent, while they both were attending the University of California at Los Angeles. They married and had three children. A difficult first birth produced a girl, but she did not survive. Kevin was born in 1954, and Winona was born in 1956.[24] Patricia devoted her time to caring for her two children and raising them the Lakota way. She was a gentle mother and never raised her voice. She would often sing to her children, and if they were fussing, fighting, or behaving badly, she would leave them in a room and tell them to come out when they were ready to get along. Kevin and Winona's maternal grandparents were always around when they were in California, so the two children were able to spend a lot of quality time with them.[25]

Like her own mother and father, Patricia moved around a lot due to Ned's job. He worked for the Systems Development Corporation and did contract work for the US military. He set up defense monitoring systems that were designed to give an early warning of any possible Russian airstrikes to the US mainland during the Korean War.

Ned provided a stable income for the family, while Patricia would help earn extra money only if she could have her children by her side. She worked at local YMCAs and YWCAs in Los Angeles, California; Great Falls, Montana; and Anchorage, Alaska. These were very popular community and recreational centers back then. They offered opportunities to learn new skills, and Patricia taught swimming, tennis, guitar, aerobics, and dance such as ballet, interpretive, ethnic, and ballroom. She put to good use all the lessons she had learned in her childhood.

This is one of the reasons learning new skills is so valuable; you never know when they will come in handy.

Even though Ned was a protective and supportive father, all the required relocation because of his work caused friction in his and Patricia's marriage, and they finally divorced each other. It is always sad when parents divorce, and some children mistakenly blame themselves for their parents' separation. In reality, divorce is never a child's fault. Sometimes parents try to stay together, but their marriage still doesn't work out.

Patricia made the best of the situation and never complained or spoke ill of her children's father. Some kids like it when their parents are separated because they no longer have to witness any more fighting and they have a calmer environment to live in. Patricia always made sure her children understood that their parents loved them, and Kevin would go and visit his father no matter where he lived.[26]

4 / Warrior

Patricia and her family had moved to Anchorage, Alaska for Ned's job in 1966. With Patricia still in Alaska after the divorce, an opportunity appeared that she thought she would like to try. After all, Kevin and Winona were teenagers now and didn't need her as much as they had when they were younger, and this opportunity would help shape her future.

The opportunity presented itself when Patricia noticed that the Indigenous people moving from the villages to Anchorage faced many challenges as they tried to adjust to city life. In the villages, they had lived according to their Indian ways and had spoken their own languages. Moving to a city like Anchorage, however, was similar to moving to a foreign country. Anyone would have trouble moving to a place where they couldn't speak the language and didn't know the customs. They would need to learn new skills to be able to survive, and Patricia saw that the Indigenous people were interested in learning how to live in the city.

She thought about how she could help the Indigenous population be more successful in the city, and an idea came to her. She would open a place where the people could get help with filling out applications for jobs, schooling, housing, and medical and dental referrals, and where they could find a little bit of companionship. In 1967, Patricia opened the Anchorage Welcome Center for Indians, Eskimos, and Aleuts.[27]

Many of the people Patricia was helping spoke only their own Native languages, and she admired them for their faithfulness to their mother tongue. Patricia's mother spoke Lakota, and her father spoke Chippewa. However, she had not learned either language. Instead, she and her family spoke English at home.[28]

Patricia realized that, because of her family and educational background, she could help both the white inhabitants of Anchorage and the villagers understand the issues each one faced. She had a gift of interpreting what another person was trying to express, and she would demonstrate this gift over and over throughout her life. Language became less of a barrier as Patricia used love, patience, and humor to facilitate communication between people of different cultures.

Here is an example of how the city's residents, who had permanent housing, and the village people who had just arrived in the city thought in different ways. The welcome center only operated during the day and did not have places for sleeping.

The post office, on the other hand, was left open all the time so that the people who were working night shifts could get their mail whenever their shift ended.

Many Indigenous village people, upon moving to the city, decided to use the post office as a place to sleep until they could find more permanent housing. The city's residents did not like this, as they no longer felt safe when getting their mail. So the postal authorities decided the post office would no longer be open twenty-four hours. They locked the post office at night and didn't care that the villagers didn't have a place to sleep. The residents of the city felt that closing the post office at night solved the problem. But now where would the homeless village people go to sleep? That issue had not been resolved.[29]

In contrast, the Indigenous people operated on a different value system. The villagers would have taken care of every person, and they would have been happy to use a public building that had the space to give people shelter. Patricia set about convincing other like-minded city residents to help. They put their minds together and found another place where the villagers could have a warm meal and place to gather five days a week. That was the best they could do at the time.

Patricia, with Kevin and Winona by her side, provided these comforts for the countless villagers who came through. Their small family didn't have much money at the time, but it didn't matter, as they were willing to sacrifice their material comforts to help others. This is the Indigenous way. Unfortunately, the welcome center did not continue to operate after Patricia left Anchorage.

Nowadays, on freezing cold nights, some US cities such as Seattle open public buildings for countless homeless people to sleep in. Some even provide cots and blankets. These same cities offer public buildings as a place to cool down from the heat as well. They are called "cooling centers." It is good to care for the well-being of all people.

True to her Lakota culture and upbringing, while Patricia was still in Alaska, her warrior skills were unleashed with the next project she undertook. To understand her path of service, it is important to note that the philosophy of leadership is different in Indian culture. Strong leaders are known for their concern and for helping others. Leadership means putting people first and not merely making promises but actually serving people. This kind of leadership is based on honesty and truthfulness, and these qualities are what the Lakota honor and revere in a strong leader. These qualities make someone a warrior. The term *warrior* has been misunderstood in white culture. Before there were reservations (prior to 1851), the term *akíčhita* (warrior) in the Lakota language was used to describe an individual who served in various altruistic organizations, or *okȟólakičhiye*. This selfless person was dedicated to performing services for the greater good of the people, and he would even sacrifice his own life if needed. The service organizations were eventually dismantled by the US government, and the term came to mean those who enlisted in the US military.[30]

Today, the term *warrior* is known more for its overarching universal spiritual meaning of "one who has given up his own ego and devotes his life to the betterment and protection of the community." Patricia was a warrior for society.[31]

Patricia had met so many people when she was working at the welcome center that it was inevitable that she would learn of a horrible, little-known fact. When Alaska became the forty-ninth state in January of 1959, there was still much to be worked out between the Indigenous peoples and the majority-white governing bodies. The little-known fact is that when Russia sold Alaska to the United States, there was an article—titled Article III—in the treaty with Russia, which was dated March 30, 1867. The article clearly states that the Aboriginal or Indigenous peoples of Alaska would enjoy all the rights and protections of the law provided to all citizens of the United States.[32]

In 1967, this promise was still not being fulfilled, and the Indigenous people were experiencing many injustices.

Native leaders came to Patricia to ask her for advice. True to her heritage, she began speaking out against this injustice and advocating for the rights of the Indigenous peoples of Alaska. She would go to hearings or meetings where a formal discussion was being held to decide the fate of the Indian peoples, and she would speak on their behalf. She was always prepared—more prepared than her opponents—with facts so that she could convince lawmakers to listen to her arguments.[33]

Arguments here means presenting facts and reasons as to why something ought to be done. By providing arguments, Patricia could convince or persuade others of the accuracy and justice of her views. This type of argument is different from an angry quarrel. Of course, since Patricia was so thorough in her preparation and knowledge of the facts, she probably did make some people angry, as she was always right. They probably found her intimidating. They may have never heard an Indian woman, or any woman for that matter, present her arguments with such force as this Lakota woman. Patricia was able to present her views passionately without yelling, and then she could turn around and make her enemies her friends with her gifts of understanding and reasoning.

Whenever Patricia spoke out against the injustices experienced by the Indigenous peoples of Alaska, she was teaching them how to speak up for their rights, as well as the rights of others. To the Indigenous people she became a mentor, an aunt, and a grandparent. While she was instrumental in working for American Indian rights in Alaska, she was knowledgeable and could converse on a wide variety of other issues.

While Patricia was in Anchorage, she met Art Davidson and his family, and they would become good friends. They found adjoining apartments and became an extended family. Patricia was always concerned for the safety and betterment of her children, and this arrangement provided an enriching life for both families. Art became a mentor to Kevin. When the two families first met, Patricia brought Art's family a gift because, according to Lakota tradition, when you first meet a person, you bring a gift.[34]

Patricia didn't have a lot of money during this time, even though she accomplished a lot. She made do with what she had. Remember, this is a woman who had only been able to afford two sets of clothes in college. To support her family during the time when she opened the welcome center and was advocating in political venues, Patricia continued to teach swimming, guitar, and dance lessons at the YMCA. She also taught at Alaska Methodist University, which was to be the first of eight colleges where she would teach.

Now, however, she needed to look for a job with a regular income.

5 / Warriors in Training

Patricia and her children, Kevin and Winona, were very close. Just as her parents had done for her, Patricia educated them in the best way possible so that they could live in both the Lakota and the white world. Wherever they lived, she made sure they grew up in a safe and creative environment with enriching experiences. Patricia and Kevin found mentors like Art, who taught Kevin how to build a house, and Abraham End of Horn and other elders, who taught him the Lakota ways and language.[35]

Patricia loved dogs and would often pick up strays on the reservation. Dogs sometimes sense who will feed them, love them, and take care of them, and Patricia would often be taking care of five or so dogs at a time. She would always take them for walks and buy them treats and toys. She was a "dog whisperer." Kevin and Winona never had to ask if they could have a dog because there was always a few on hand.[36]

When Kevin and Winona went to college, they both attended Haskell Indian Junior College—now Haskell Indian Nations University in Lawrence, Kansas—

and the Institute of American Indian Arts in Santa Fe, New Mexico.[37] Kevin also attended Black Hills State College and later the University of North Dakota. He became a teacher just like his mother, and he was able to teach elementary school on the reservation. He liked teaching on the reservation because he could mix with the families and get to know the children better. Most of the teachers were white and did not live on the reservation, and they would rush home after school and would rarely return to participate in any evening social activities.[38]

Patricia felt a little sad that she didn't speak her Native language, and she made it a goal for others to learn theirs by promoting language preservation projects. Her enthusiasm for speaking Lakota must have rubbed off on Kevin, as he wanted to learn Lakota and was mentored by elders who knew it well. He set his goal high and learned seventeen Lakota words per day, and he now speaks Lakota proficiently.[39]

Arlo Goodbear, a member of a well-known Mandan Hidatsa dance family, taught Kevin how to Hoop Dance and encouraged him to use his dance to teach people unity and other Lakota values. Kevin quickly became proficient at Hoop Dancing, and he is now a famous, internationally known Hoop Dancer.[40]

Patricia and Winona researched all the issues that were problematic for Indians, such as the need for the US government to keep its promises and honor its treaties with Indigenous people; the need for tribes to be able to determine their own future; the need for better education for Indigenous people from kindergarten to college; the need for Native language preservation; the need for religious freedom for Indigenous people; the need to combat prejudice and racism toward Indians; and the poor treatment of Indigenous women and girls. Winona helped prepare and type the materials for her mom to use in speeches, discussions, and writings. It is good to be concerned about current issues and to help people figure out how to resolve some or parts of any problem, and Winona and Kevin would often discuss strategies that could help organizations such as the National Tribal Leaders Association and the National Congress of American Indians.[41]

Most of the problematic issues for Indians stemmed from the prejudice and racism against them that had begun a long time ago with colonization. *Colonization* is the control by one group of people over another group of people, usually outsiders. For example, a series of official edicts, called papal bulls, was issued by the pope between 1491 and 1493. One of these decrees was the Inter Cetera Bull of May 4, 1492, which was also called the Doctrine of Discovery. *Inter cetera* means "among others or among the rest."[42]

One of the salient features of the Doctrine of Discovery is that it considered Indigenous people worldwide to be savages and maintained that they had no right to own land, regardless of whether they were nomadic, hunters and gatherers, or farmers. Many Europeans wanted to claim the Indigenous people's lands, settle on them, and create their own farmsteads. Additionally, many of the whites moving into the territory at the time were farmers, and they felt that their way of working the land was superior to the Indigenous methods. Yet more than three-fifths of the crops that are now in cultivation were introduced by Indigenous people and their methods of farming. Indians have also made countless other contributions that have improved the lives of people on the planet.[43]

The Europeans also felt justified in forcing Indigenous people to discard their own religious practices, to convert to Christianity, and to stop speaking their Native languages. The Europeans who settled in Canada, the United States, and South America used residential boarding schools to indoctrinate Indigenous children, and this practice was very cruel and caused great hardship for the Indigenous people. Children were taken away from their parents and placed in these schools where their hair was cut, where their traditional clothes were taken away, and where they could not speak their Native languages. They were taught only how to perform menial tasks and very little of the subjects that are normally taught in a regular school. They were also beaten into submission and punished severely for the slightest reason. Frequently, children tried to escape and died trying to get back home. Sometimes they were killed by the school staff, who would then tell the parents that the child had run away. Much is now coming to light about the treatment of the children who were in these schools, and one can read and watch all about them online.[44]

Many people can see that the Doctrine of Discovery is outdated and offensive, but it is still used to promote the feeling of superiority of one group over another group. In 1993, Patricia mounted her steed of knowledge once again, and along with her friend, Jacqueline Left Hand Bull, attempted to dissolve once and for all the support for colonization that the Doctrine of Discovery had granted. They addressed the Parliament of Religions in Chicago with a resolution titled "American Indian

Declaration of Vision 1993." Briefly, the resolution states that Indigenous people were profoundly religious and that they had their own Messengers of God. They were not a people to be conquered and forced into another's religion or way of life. Instead, they needed to be supported, like any other people, in their efforts to preserve and maintain their languages, cultures, and religions.[45]

The resolution was well received, but it could not nullify the papal bulls. Only the pope could do this. Some people burn a copy of the Doctrine of Discovery in October on Indigenous Day, as a protest, in hopes that one day the doctrine will officially be nullified.

To prepare their arguments, Patricia and Winona needed to understand the treaties made with sovereign Indian nations between 1832 and 1871. *Treaties* are formal promises. A treaty sets up a set of rules between two parties. About 368 treaties had been made between the US government and American Indians, and most had been ratified by the US Senate. *Ratification* means that the treaties were passed and became law. Of course, some unresolved and unratified treaties also exist, and they have caused problems for Indians over the years.[46]

Though the US government, when it first signed a treaty with Indigenous people, always agreed to keep its promises, most of its treaties were not honored, and most of its promises were not kept. For example, whenever the government or a huge corporation wanted the land that belonged to a tribe, it would add an "addendum" to the treaty. In other words, the government or corporation would add different rules or use trickery to get what it wanted from the Indigenous people.

Of course, this was not fair to the Indians, who often did not know what the new rules were. Patricia didn't have to know everything about all the treaties, but she most likely had access to the treaties themselves. Patricia, Kevin, and Winona had to think like lawyers in order to stand up for the rights of Indians in court. So much preparation! It's no wonder that Winona's daughter, May, became a real lawyer. Being around her mom and her Uŋčí—grandmother—most likely influenced her.

In helping their mom with her work, Kevin and Winona were preparing themselves to be very knowledgeable so they could serve the Indigenous community and humanity as well. They were learning to be warriors!

6 / Projects Aplenty!

Patricia was a multitasker, which means she was able to work on achieving several goals at a time. For example, while she was living in Alaska, she thought of various ways to earn a regular income to support her family while she was busy helping Indigenous village people adjust to city life. She had always had a long-term goal to improve education on reservations throughout the United States, and while in Alaska, she found an opportunity to both earn money and work on that goal by interviewing for a job in Boulder, Colorado with the Western Interstate Council on Higher Education (WICHE). Patricia excitedly took the job and in 1970 moved to Boulder, Colorado to begin work.[47]

This organization set up community colleges to help students who otherwise would not be able to attend college. Often, when a young person moved away to attend a college or university, he or she would be forced to leave behind an elder—a much-loved member of the family who required home care. This situation always left the young person with having to make a difficult choice, and their Lakota values won out most of the time. The young person would not go to school and would instead stay home to care for the loved one.[48]

Patricia thought it would be a good idea if community colleges could be set up on Indian reservations. She approached her uncle—Douglas Sky, who was then the Lakota tribal chairman—with this idea. He liked it, so Patricia set about writing a proposal for her vision. A *proposal* is a plan for how to make an idea become reality.

The first community college would be constructed on the Standing Rock Reservation, and Douglas and Patricia enlisted others to help implement the plan. Standing Rock Community College in Fort Yates, North Dakota opened on September 21, 1973.[49] The name of the college was changed to Sitting Bull College in March of 1996 to honor this important Indian leader, who had resisted the US government's attempts to forcibly relocate Indigenous people onto reservations. Today, the Lakota tribe maintains control over the college so that Lakota values are upheld, and the college is still an accredited institution of higher learning, which guarantees that it has qualified teachers like any other college. Patricia knew that the college would be a success, and helping youth pursue higher education was a lifelong goal of hers.[50]

Patricia went on to encourage the building of other community colleges, and by 1972, six community colleges had been constructed on reservations. Patricia and the WICHE created the American Indian Higher Education Consortium (AIHEC) to assist with the many issues yet to be worked out for colleges on reservations. A *consortium* is a group of two or more people or organizations that work together to achieve a common goal.[51]

All colleges on the reservations were accredited. At first, these colleges offered only associate degrees and certificates, but today, some offer bachelor's and master's degrees. These colleges are helpful for people who want a smaller school, a different cultural experience, and a family environment that comes from remaining close to home. Most of these schools are open to anyone—whether Indigenous or not—who wishes to apply to them. Patricia personally assisted seventeen tribes with establishing community colleges on their reservations. Today, many more such colleges have been built.[52]

Patricia believed that the tribes needed to have control over their schools and that they would need to be able to determine the curriculum that would be used. She brought these points to federal, state, and city government officials and advocated on behalf of different tribes. She wanted all people, especially those in these different levels of government, to recognize and protect tribal sovereign rights, and no matter how much opposition she encountered, she kept her focus on gaining sovereignty for Indigenous tribes.

Fortunately, in 1975, the Indian Self-Determination and Education Assistance Act gave tribal governments the ability to exercise their sovereignty and to have control over their own affairs. An *act* is a law passed by a legislature.

In 1824, Congress had given the Bureau of Indian Affairs the duty of subjugating and assimilating American Indians. *Assimilation* is when an individual or group of people from a different heritage acquire, through compulsion or voluntarily, the mode of life of a dominant culture.

Now, with the Indian Self-Determination and Education Assistance Act, Congress changed direction and allowed tribes to "contract" different services they wanted, such as resource management, law enforcement, education, childcare, and environmental protection. This act promoted Indian self-determination because tribes were now able to manage their own affairs more fully by choosing what services to request. However, the BIA still had to approve each tribe's contract.

There were some barriers to this process. For instance, tribes could not reallocate funds if they had a need for more funds in another area of their budget. *Reallocate* means that you take funds from one part of your budget you aren't using and place them in another part you are using more. Despite these deficiencies, Patricia, along with others, lobbied members of Congress hard on the passage of the Self-Determination Act.

The policy of the US government toward American Indians is unnecessarily complex. For example, Congress has often added amendments to laws relating to Indigenous people. *Amendments* are the additions to the law that provide specifics and make them constitutional again. These amendments—like the additions to treaties made with Indians—were always designed to give an advantage to non-Indians without considering the effect they would have on Indians.

Working with WICHE gave Patricia many opportunities to serve Indigenous people and improve their lives. She was able to connect with lots of people, and here are just a few examples of the goals she was able to accomplish.

In 1975, she was the keynote speaker to the Native American Teacher Training Program at St. Regis Mohawk Reservation and spoke on the topic "Competency-Based Native American Education."[53]

In 1977, she was elected president of the National Indian Education Association.[54]

In 1978, she was appointed Director of WICHE Planning Resources in Minority Education. She wrote a well-received paper titled "A Survey of College and University Programs for American Indians."[55]

In 1978, she assisted in passing the HR 11104 Tribally Controlled Community College Assistance Act.[56]

In 1979, she was appointed co-chair-woman of the Department of the Interior Task Force of Indian Education Policy.[57]

In 1982, she represented the United States in education discussions at the World Assembly of First Nations in Saskatchewan, Canada.[58]

In 1989, she co-authored a paper with Dean Chavers titled "The Effects of Testing on Native Americans," which was sponsored by the National Commission on Testing and Public Policy.[59]

In 1990, she gave a presentation—for which we have a summary—on the Lakota view of the child at the University of Southern Maine.[60]

Another milestone Patricia, while doing all her work for WICHE, helped achieve was the passage of the 1978 Religious Freedom Act. Before 1978, American Indians in the United States could not legally practice their religions, and Congress often passed laws that allowed US soldiers to imprison or even kill Indigenous people who were carrying out their tribal ceremonies. Since the mid-1800s, Indian religions had been outlawed. Patricia herself recalled that when she was very young, her parents would take her to sun dances, which were considered illegal by the US government. Her parents could have been fired from the BIA on the spot if anyone had discovered they were attending Indian ceremonies, and Patricia had been instructed, at three years old, not to tell anyone that she had been, or was going to, a sun dance. Of course, children like to talk and share experiences, so it must have been very difficult for Patricia and her sister to be quiet about such things. Still, the girls listened to their parents, and consequently no harm came to them.[61]

Patricia believed that Indigenous people should also have the freedom to practice their own religion. After all, this was a right enshrined in the Constitution for everyone else. She, along with a few others, worked on getting the American

Indian Religious Freedom Act passed. She wrote much of the language in the bill, and she began working on it during the time she was setting up community colleges on Indian reservations. She spent a lot of time away from home in Washington, DC, talking with members of Congress.

On August 11, 1978, the American Indian Religious Freedom Act was passed and became Public Law 95-341.[62] A *law* is a set of rules and standards set by the government. This passage of the American Indian Religious Freedom Act meant that American Indians could carry out their ceremonies and pray freely in the manner to which they were accustomed.

Patricia and her colleagues wanted to end prejudicial policies related to American Indians and reservations once and for all, and getting this bill signed into law was a very important step.[63]

The American Indian Religious Freedom Act lasted until 1988—a total of ten years—before it was struck down by the Supreme Court.[64] That meant it was no

longer a law and was considered unconstitutional. Today, it remains on the books but is not enforceable. For example, in 1988, the Forest Service at the Six Rivers National Forest, Chimney Rock area, was allowed to build a road through a site that had been sacred to Indigenous people for thousands of years. The Yurok, Karok, and Tolowa tribes of California filed the Lyng vs. NW Indian Cemetery Protective Association lawsuit that eventually reached the Supreme Court, and the court sided with the state of California even though an alternative route existed that would have allowed the road to pass around the sacred site without desecrating it. Soon after the ruling, the Forest Service built the road through the site so a lumber company could harvest trees.[65]

This outcome disappointed Patricia very much. Once again, there was no religious freedom for Indigenous people on Turtle Island.

In February of 1993, Patricia was appointed by the Association on American Indian Affairs, Inc. to be the Coordinator of the Coalition for the Amendments to the American Indian Religious Freedom Act (AIRFA).[66] This involved managing some sixty-five organizations with the goal of making and passing amendments that would be clear and would protect Indigenous Religious rights. This was no simple task, and Patricia became even more known for her skill in getting people to work together. In April of 1993, she was also elected to the National Spiritual Assembly, which we will talk more about later.

The American Indian Religious Freedom Act had two amendments, one in 1994 (HR4155) and one in 1996 (HR4230). Patricia was invited to help write the 1996 law, and Public Law 95-341 thus became constitutional again.

Another project Patricia undertook was the preservation of Indigenous languages. She often traveled to Washington,

DC, to lobby for the preservation of these languages. As usual, she would prepare herself with all the facts she could gather, and she did not back down in the face of opposition. She teamed up with two Indigenous language enthusiasts—Harlene Green, a Cherokee grant writer who was focused on preserving the Cherokee language, and LaDonna Harris, a Comanche social activist and politician.[67]

In 1990, the Native American Language Act, which made it possible for Indians to use their Native language in school, was passed.[68] In the past, Indian children would have their mouths washed out with lye soap or would be beaten for speaking their language. Now books could be written in Native languages, and the passage of this act made Patricia very happy.

In addition to these accomplishments, Patricia helped Indigenous people throughout the Pacific Islands preserve their languages. In 1999, she became the President of Pacific and American Indigenous Language Survival, Inc.[69]

Patricia also had an interest in preserving sacred Indigenous sites, and she had been saddened by the desecration of the sacred Indigenous site at the Six Rivers National Forest. Gary Kimble, an attorney who was also Indigenous, invited her to work on a project to protect sacred sites in

New York. Gary was the project director, and the goal of the project was to ensure that Indigenous people retained their ceremonial sites so they could practice their sacred rites.

It was a big challenge to keep the sacred sites from being used for multiple purposes. For example, some of the land was being used for grazing cattle, for growing wheat, and for logging. The project team had to receive permission to practice the sacred rites from many different entities, including the Forest Service, the Bureau of Land Management, and at times, the ranchers and farmers leasing the land. Different tribes had different thoughts on how to preserve the land they all used for ceremonies, and the team also had to work with twenty to thirty tribes to get a consensus for practicing the sacred rites. No wonder it took years for Patricia and Gary to get anything done, and hats off to their team for having the patience for this work. At times, it was daunting.[70]

The team also worked on retrieving sacred artifacts that had been stolen and placed in museums or private collections. Because of their efforts, some of these objects were eventually returned to their rightful owners.[71]

Finally, the project team was successful in getting the prison system to allow medicine men to visit Indigenous prisoners. Many other Indigenous practices, however, did not receive approval for prisoners due to the restrictions of prison life.[72]

7 / Home at Last!

In 1983, Patricia sold her house in Boulder, Colorado and moved onto the Standing Rock Reservation on the South Dakota side. Kevin had already moved back onto the reservation. Patricia's mother was originally from Standing Rock, but she no longer lived there, and Patricia moved without having a house to live in.[73] Patricia and her daughter, Winona, and three grandchildren lived in a tent on the reservation or an apartment in Mobridge, the adjacent town.[74]

Patricia didn't mind the hardship. She wanted to be on the reservation to be near her people, the culture, the language, and to attend activities such as the pow-wows, celebrations, festivals, dinners, and sun dances. She could now experience the changing of the seasons, hear the winds rustling through the cottonwood trees, and feel the heat of the fire pits warming up the rocks prepared for an *Inípi*, which was a ceremony for purification using steam created by heated rocks. She could also smell the sage and sweetgrass at ceremonies, and she would pray by bringing the smoke toward her face with her hands, wafting it over her head, and directing it toward her heart. This ritual is called smudging, or, in Lakota, *Azílya*. The White Buffalo Calf Woman set the example of how to use Azílya to invoke purity, sanctity, and holiness.[75]

Patricia, like most Indians on Standing Rock, enjoyed bitterroot. In Lakota it is called *Siŋkphé tȟa-wóyute*, and it is used for colds and a sore throat. She also liked Indian or wild turnip, which has a few common names in English, such as bog onion or brown dragon. In Lakota, it is called *Thíŋpsila*. She liked it because it didn't raise her blood sugar the way potatoes did. On special occasions, she would enjoy an Indian taco made with frybread. To her, the reservation was home.

In 1987, Kevin was able to acquire a house. Then a few years later, Patricia was able to purchase her own home on a high point overlooking the confluence of the Missouri and Grand rivers within Wakpala District near what the tribe called "the singing bridge."[76] This was to be her home, and she was thrilled. She didn't mind that she would have to drive a hundred miles to go to Bismarck, North Dakota, or Aberdeen, South Dakota to catch planes to travel to her Washington, DC, meetings. She had to drive to the airport so often that one of her grandchildren, Kimimila, thought she lived there.[77]

One thing for sure, now that Patricia had a home on the reservation, her dedication to language and cultural preservation, Indian rights, and education—all with Indigenous youth in mind—increased dramatically. She worked even harder to help change laws and the way people think about Indians.

Patricia would often call Indian policy meetings in her home on the reservation. She wanted the non-Indians who worked with her to experience being on the reservation for themselves. Then they would have a better understanding of Indigenous life. Patricia was a gracious hostess and made everyone comfortable and happy.[78]

8 / Her Joy!

There was nothing that gave Patricia more joy than her grandchildren, all of whom she cared for deeply. They delighted her, and she loved spending time with them. They were the reason she strove to make changes in the world. She wanted to leave behind a kinder, more just society for them. Rather than send them away when she was busy or when she was with important people, she included them. To her, *they* were the most important people. When she was alive, Patricia got to know

three granddaughters—Kimimila, Waniya, and Maymangwa—and three grandsons—Duta, Hepana, and Ohíyes'a. A
seventh grandchild, Patricia, was born on
November 17, 2010 and was named in
honor of her grandmother.[79]

Patricia would occasionally take one of
her grandchildren on one of her business
trips. Waniya remembers that her grandmother always made sure they learned
about other cultures and peoples rather
than just sightseeing and shopping. She
also made arrangements for them to meet
local people so they could get an inside
view and mix with them as members of
one family—the human family. What fun

it was for them to be visiting new grand-
mas, grandpas, aunties, uncles, and cousins, sisters, and brothers! After all, this is
the Lakota way.[80]

Patricia loved to cook for her family
and often prepared feasts for them. Any
occasion would do, whether it be someone getting a good grade on a report card,
receiving an athletic award, or some other
special event. She loved to watch her children eat. Ohíyes'a said she would prepare
meals from goulash, turkey, and wild rice,
which was grown in Minnesota, the home
of Patricia's father. Ohíyes'a loved his
grandmother's cooking. She would not
allow the children to drink liquids while

eating food, nor would she allow them to eat a lot of candy and cake. He remembers that she would sing to them all the time.[81]

Ohíyes'a also remembers that Patricia would encourage him and his cousins to put together puzzles to "stimulate" their brains. And, of course, he recalls the many

dogs. There would always be two or three dogs outside and at least as many inside.[82] Another way in which Patricia showed her love for her grandchildren was by watching basketball or other sports on television so that she could talk with her grandsons about sports. Other than this, she didn't watch television.[83]

She had a special way of calming her grandchildren down when they were fussing and fighting with each other during mealtimes. Whenever she heard them arguing, she would put a stop to it by making them eat their meal in silence. Like most children, her grandchildren did not like having to remain silent for a long period of time, so they quickly learned to cooperate with each other. Patricia wanted her grandchildren to learn how to use silence and contemplation to deal with their frustrations, as annoyances and disappointments are a part of life.[84]

Patricia's grandchildren were adults when she passed away, and they didn't know much about her many projects to improve the lives of Indigenous people. At that time, they had been children and had only noticed that they were the center of her life. Being the center of a family's life is what children are supposed to notice when they are growing up, and Patricia's grandchildren were surprised to read of her many accomplishments that improved their lives and the lives of others. Initially, they may have been surprised at the many people who admired their grandmother, yet because they knew her, they knew the admiration for her was well deserved. They were very grateful and so proud that she was their Uŋčí, and now, like the rest of the world, they are able to celebrate her accomplishments.[85]

9 / The Singing Bridge

The town of Wakpala is an Indian town on the Standing Rock reservation, and it is separated from Mobridge, a predominantly white neighborhood, by Lake Oahe. The "singing bridge" connects them. When driving on this bridge, it is best to turn the radio off, open the window, and listen to what sounds like a large group of Indians singing under the bridge. Technically, the cause of this phenomenon is probably the interaction between materials with which the bridge was built, the sound of the tires of an automobile hitting the concrete, and the ambience of the natural surroundings of rolling hills and water.

In any case, the experience makes your spirit soar. You want to turn around and drive over the bridge again and again.

In many ways, Patricia resembled this bridge. She could be friends with anyone, even with those who had opinions that differed from hers, and she was known for her ability to understand both the white and Indian sides of problems that arose between the two cultures. After all, her parents had prepared her for living in both the Indian and the white world.

Patricia became friends with the owner and publisher of the Mobridge Tribune, the local weekly newspaper. The owner, Larry Atkinson, was concerned about the racism in Mobridge toward Indians, and he invited Patricia to write articles that could educate the people about Lakota culture. Patricia respectfully turned him down, as she was so busy with her many projects. Then one day, one of her granddaughters, who was attending a mostly white elementary school in Mobridge, came home and asked, "Grandma, what's a whore?" She told her grandma that her teacher had told her class that all Indians were whores. Patricia was livid and decided she would

immediately begin writing articles for the paper. The year was 1987.[86]

Patricia wrote more than forty articles sharing the Lakota views of religion, culture, expectations for male / female behavior, and family. She also wrote about

the Lakota tribe's political status and history, and she became a "singing bridge" between the communities of Wakpala and Mobridge. Her gift of understanding different cultures was her song, and she was singing to all who would listen.[87]

In her articles, Patricia gave many examples of the differences between Indigenous and white culture. For example, one of the things she shared about her culture was the Lakota handshake. In Lakota culture, if there is even a handshake at all, it is short and gentle. In contrast, white people generally like a firm grip. When talking, the Lakota people like lots of distance between the participants, while white people prefer eight inches or closer. Lakota people also consider it rude and aggressive to stare directly into another person's eyes, but white people consider it respectful to maintain eye contact while talking.

She also explained the *give-away*, which in Lakota culture is a way to honor people and friendships on an important occasion.[88] According to Lakota values, a person accumulates wealth in order to give it away to others, not only to accumulate it for its own sake. Patricia also described the Lakota concept of *wait time*. Wait time is the practice of pausing and thinking—sometimes for days—on what a proper response should be to a question. Some people mistakenly think that such a long waiting period is a sign that a person is not very bright, while the Lakota believe it signifies that a person is giving sincere and honest thought to an issue or personal statement.[89]

Explaining the differences between Indigenous and white cultures was one way in which Patricia gave the gift of understanding.

10 / Becoming Bahá'í

Youth can teach adults important things. Never forget this. Here is an example of a son teaching his mother something very important.

When he was a youth, Kevin became a member of the Bahá'í Faith in 1979, and he told his mother about his decision to become a Bahá'í. In 1990, Patricia also became a Bahá'í. A Bahá'í is someone who believes in Bahá'u'lláh and accepts His teachings as the most recent guidance from God. God has sent a number of Divine Messengers for the entire world about every thousand or so years.

Patricia had worked long and hard to preserve American Indian religions, and she knew a lot about them. She herself believed that a Divine Messenger—the White Buffalo Calf Woman—had been sent specifically to the Lakota people and that she had promised to return. In fact, a recording exists of Patricia discussing her belief in the White Buffalo Calf Woman in a talk titled *Native American Women's Wisdom: Our Spiritual Selves*, at the 1993 Parliament of the World's Religions in Chicago. You will find the link to the website given in the endnote for this paragraph. Both Kevin and Patricia believe that Bahá'u'lláh, in addition to fulfilling the prophecies of other faiths, was the return of the White Buffalo Calf Woman, and below is how Kevin educated his mother about his belief in the Bahá'í Faith.[90]

In 1988, Kevin was invited to be a part of a teaching team called the "Trail of Light." Bahá'í Indians from North America planned to visit Indians from South America, mainly in Bolivia and Peru. Originally, the team was supposed to be an all-Bahá'í teaching team. However, because Kevin loved his mom so much and enjoyed traveling with her, he invited her to come along, and she read-ily accepted. She was an avid cigarette smoker, so in preparation for the trip, she stopped smoking so she could climb the steep trails to reach some of the villages and not embarrass Kevin. The goal of the teaching team was to travel to the remote villages where the majority of the Indigenous Bahá'í communities were located.

The team flew from South Dakota to Santa Cruz, Bolivia, where they were taken to the outskirts of the city and were given a greeting like no other. Eighty children danced and sang for them, and when it was time for the Americans to perform, the children were very excited and treated them as if they were rock stars.[91]

Of course, the sights, sounds, smells, and even the foods were different. The members of the teaching team were excited to try new things and have new experiences. Everything was different—the season was the opposite of what it was in South Dakota, and even the positions of the sun and stars were different. As for the Big Dipper, the team could only see two stars of it in Bolivia. The team members loved trying the different fruits—cherimoya, guanabana, guayaba, jicama, mamoncillo, and tamarindo—and they ate so many varieties of potatoes they lost count. However, Patricia couldn't eat the fried llama. She recalled the llamas' big, soft brown eyes, and that put an end to that experience.[92]

Since the team had been supplied with excellent interpreters, they could communicate with their Quechua and Aymara-speaking hosts. They were so glad to be on this trip, as there are so many more Indigenous people in South America than in the United States. Patricia considered it "Indian heaven" and was quite moved that the people considered her and the group to be their relatives—which of course, as members of one human family, they were.[93]

The team was then flown to Sucre, Bolivia. Sixty Indians were waiting to meet them, and they greeted the team in the special Quechua way, which is to shake hands and then briefly grab or grip the other person's shoulders. This was different than the Lakota greeting, where the hand is held lightly and is then followed with a short pump. Patricia loved the Quechua greeting.[94]

Then the team went on a six-hour car ride to the remote Peruvian village Mayu. The road—which we would most likely call a trail—was long, steep, and winding. The journey was scary because there was no room for two cars, yet vehicles were constantly coming from both directions. Their car seemed to be constantly on the precipice and ready to fall off, and Patricia would often close her eyes and talk a lot to calm herself.[95]

The next village the team visited was Misque Pampa. The journey there was a nine-hour drive and was even more treacherous than the drive to Mayu. The team needed several breaks to stretch their legs. As they neared the village, they could see and hear around eighty Indians lining the road singing a welcome song. Everyone stood in a line and greeted each of the team members with "Alláh-u-Abhá!" This phrase is an Arabic term for "God is the Most Glorious," and Bahá'ís use it to greet one another. Since Patricia wasn't a Bahá'í, this greeting must have sounded strange to her ears. So, she just said, "Hello!"

Somewhere, as Patricia moved down the line of people, something inside her changed. The Indians were greeting the team with so much love and respect that Patricia could not contain herself! By the time she reached the end of the line, she was also saying "Alláh-u-Abhá" with tears in her eyes. Her heart had been moved by all the love. Her spirit recognized Who Bahá'u'lláh was, and the team could see and feel the transformation in her. That was the beginning of something very grand in Patricia's life.[96]

Patricia studied the Bahá'í Faith for a few years. She asked questions of Kevin and their friend Jacqueline Left Hand Bull, and for a time, Patricia thought that these were the only two Bahá'ís she knew. She asked Kevin to introduce her to some Bahá'ís in the United States, and she hadn't realized that most of Kevin's friends were Bahá'ís and that she had already met quite a few of them—including a couple of judges, Dorothy and James Nelson. Patricia dearly admired these two already. She and Dorothy had both gone to UCLA at the same time and were interested in law and civil rights.

Kevin invited Patricia to a National Bahá'í Convention in Wilmette, Illinois, and he told her that she could meet lots of Bahá'ís there in the hotel lobby. When she wondered why she couldn't go to the sessions, Kevin explained to her that they were for Bahá'ís only—not because there were any secrets but so that the Bahá'ís could speak frankly about any issues that would be presented. Patricia asked how she could get into the sessions, and Kevin told her she would have to become a Bahá'í. When Patricia asked how she could do this, Kevin presented her with an enrollment card. You use an enrollment card to formally enroll in the Bahá'í community and to let others know that you want to take this path. Patricia completed the card and handed it back to Kevin, who then took it to someone who could officially add her. She was allowed into the sessions.[97]

Becoming Bahá'í—as Linda Covey, a friend of Patricia's, would say—is a process. In Patricia's case, her heart accepted Bahá'u'lláh in that very remote village of Misque Pampa, where the villagers were so enamored with Bahá'u'lláh that their love for Him completely washed over her. She knew the strength of this love by those villagers who lived up to the teachings of the Bahá'í Faith. Patricia continued learning more and more about this religion from her son and from reading about it.

So there you have it—Kevin the son introduced Patricia the mother to something life-changing.

Keeping the teachings and traditions of her Lakota culture prepared Patricia for becoming a Bahá'í. When she accepted Bahá'u'lláh as a Manifestation of God, she never gave up who she was, or her culture, or her past lessons. After all, the Lakota teachings consider everyone to be family, and the same is true for the Bahá'í Faith. With the coming of a more recent Messenger of God, Bahá'u'lláh, some of the teachings from previous Messengers were updated to reflect the age in which we live, and a new spiritual remedy for the world's ills was given to humanity.

One new teaching Patricia learned was *consultation*. Remember, her parents wanted her to learn to live in both the Indian and white world. In the white world, especially in political and some other circles, people use confrontation and bullying to get what they want. For example, whenever Patricia traveled to Washington, DC, to advocate for the rights of Indians, she believed that she had to use these forms of manipulation—all of which she was excellent at—to achieve the results she wanted. With this kind of adversarial process, people think that they must win arguments before peace and unity is achieved.

In the Bahá'í Faith, consultation begins with absolute harmony, love, and cooperation among those who are going to work together to achieve a collective action. There is no need for arguing or browbeating; instead, there is full and frank discussion. For example, once a person states his opinion, it is no longer his but instead belongs to the group. This way, the group—not the individual—owns the idea and decision. Differences of opinion during consultation, therefore, are not to be taken personally. Everyone needs to be heard, regardless of whether someone is rich, poor, educated, uneducated, Black, white, or Indigenous. In fact, a diverse group will often provide different angles of an idea that can be heard, and these diverse viewpoints will likely result in a better outcome than if everyone held the same opinion.

Patricia, who was known for her honesty and justness, felt this form of consultation freed up her heart and mind so that she could be free to do her best work. Whenever she served as the chairperson of a meeting, she quickly learned how to move people through some rather difficult consultations. Those working with her found her leadership style refreshing. She incorporated storytelling into consultations whenever she could, and her stories often lightened the atmosphere.

Whenever she wanted to get a point across to others, she always had a story ready. She did not like boastful people or people full of themselves, and here is one story she would tell about self-importance.

Once a land turtle who couldn't swim was trapped on a small island with rapidly rising waters. Two eagles were flying by, saw his plight, and warned the turtle he was about to drown. The turtle said, "You could save me." When they asked how, the turtle told them to get a large stick. Each eagle would grab one end of the stick in its talons. Then the turtle would clamp his jaws down on the middle of the stick, and the two eagles would fly away with the turtle hanging on. The two eagles did as the turtle had asked, and the plan worked well. They were flying away when another eagle was flying by and said, "What a brilliant idea! Whose idea was that?" The turtle could not resist. He opened his mouth to say, "Miiiiinnne" and let go of the stick, plunging into the swirling waters below.[98]

Patricia had plenty of opportunity to practice the art of consultation, for in 1993 she was elected to the National Spiritual Assembly of the Bahá'ís of the United

States. This shocked her because she was such a new Bahá'í, but those around her helped her with the new role.

She was able to travel and, along with the Nelsons and Juana Conrad, represented the National Spiritual Assembly at the Fourth International Women's Conference that was held in Beijing, China in 1995. Patricia was elected chairperson of the Indigenous Women's Caucus. She proved to be quite successful at chairing this caucus, as she knew all the issues and could lead intelligently because of it.[99]

One of Patricia's favorite Bahá'ís was Hand of the Cause Rúhiyyih Khánum, whom she met in 1994 when the entire National Spiritual Assembly was invited to go to Haifa, Israel, where the international center of the Bahá'í Faith is located. At the meeting, Rúhiyyih Khánum invited Patricia to sit next to her as a sign of respect for Indigenous people.

Rúhíyyih Khánum had been given the title *Hand of the Cause,* which is an appointment for life, and her main functions were to teach and protect the Bahá'í Faith. She loved Indigenous people and would often travel to give them the message of Bahá'u'lláh directly. She was Canadian by birth and was used to all sorts of comforts, yet she traveled to distant places, such as the Amazon rainforest, to teach the people there about Bahá'u'lláh. She also spent time helping the Bahá'ís of Canada and the United States understand why it was important to include Indigenous people in their consultations. She and Patricia became fast and inseparable friends. When Rúhiyyih Khánum died in 2000, Patricia was heartbroken, and she was at a loss. She would cry, "Who is going to stand up for the Indigenous people?" This proved to be one of Patricia's most heartrending moments, and such moments seemed to be occurring more often in her life now.[100]

11 / The 'Abhá Kingdom Welcomes Patricia

With the passing of Rúhíyyih <u>Khá</u>-num in 2000 and the terrible automobile accident that claimed the life of Patricia's grandson, Hepana, in 1999, Patricia's health began to decline. She had been diagnosed with diabetes, and now it was affecting the circulation in her legs. In the summer of 2001, after a Bahá'í conference in Milwaukee, Patricia became ill.[101] She was now seventy-three years old. Her cousin, Robert End of Horn, Sr., had invited her to a pow-wow, and she had attended in a wheelchair. Kevin wheel-danced with her on the pow-wow floor, and they were soon playing an honor song for Patricia. Everyone was showing her gratitude for her warmth, kindness, and service. It was to be her last pow-wow.[102]

When Patricia was invited to the San Carlos Apache Reservation near Globe, Arizona, she also attended using her wheelchair. At first, she had declined to go, but the host had insisted that she come. She attended but became sick from something she ate before coming to the event. That night, she went to the hospital, and the doctors found that her diabetes had progressed to the point that both her legs needed to be amputated up to the knees. During this time, she was sedated, with all kinds of tubes attached to her. Kevin and Winona were by her side at the hospital when she passed away on October 20, 2001.[103]

Frances, her younger sister, passed away fifteen years after Patricia did, and Patricia is now with Eva, John, Frances, and her beloved grandson, Hepana. One can only imagine her elation at being with Rúhíyyih Khánum in the 'Abhá Kingdom, which is another term for "heaven."

At her funeral, hundreds of people from all walks of life came to pay their respects. The Standing Rock Radio station, KLDN, broadcast the entire funeral for three hours so that those who couldn't make it would be able to participate. Ťhawáčhiŋ Wašté Wiŋ, or Compassionate Woman, was loved by all. She left this world a better place for her grandchildren and for all grandchildren.[104]

She loved the Bahá'í youth so much that her final written words from her hospital bed were "To the Bahá'í Youth of the World: We come to you in loving consultation." As you will recall, Patricia incorporated her Lakota ways—which were already a part of her life—into all her consultations, and she became a role model in mastering this decision-making process. Consultation frees people to speak the truth as they see it, to be themselves without fear of judgment, to independently investigate the truth, and to collectively create something beautiful and fresh through the participation of everyone involved. Patricia wished for all youth to be able to participate and cooperate in their decision-making in order to make this world a better place.[105]

Youth, you are the hope of the world, and Patricia has given you the example of how she led her life as a way for you to move forward in order to continue the work of uniting all the races into one fam-

ily and to care for the environment and planet.

From the bottom of our hearts, thank you, Patricia, for all you have done!

12 / Distinctions

Patricia was not one to seek out notoriety. She worked diligently to advance causes she believed would help all people—both Indian and non-Indian—but she never aspired to receive any recompense for her service to humanity. However, people often honored her anyway, as they felt she deserved special recognition for her service.

In 1970, at age forty-two, Patricia received her Lakota name. Amos Dog

Eagle had the responsibility of finding her a Lakota name, and after he prayed and fasted for several days, he knew what her name would be. It would be "Thawáčhiŋ Wašté Wiŋ" which, as you recall, means "Compassionate Woman." It was quite an honor for Patricia to receive her Lakota name.[106]

In 1991, Patricia received the MacArthur Fellowship Award, which is given by the John D. and Catherine T. MacArthur Foundation to US citizens who show exceptional merit and promise for continued and enhanced creative work. You can't apply for this award; someone must nominate you. Then a team at the Foundation reviews each nomination and decides who will receive the award. Frequently, as in the case with Patricia, you receive a congratulatory phone call, and this is when you know you will receive the award.

You can imagine that Patricia was very surprised when she received the phone call congratulating her. The award is given along with money that is distributed to the recipient over a number of years to carry out future creative work. Patricia used this money to further preserve Lakota language and culture.[107]

In 1992, she went on pilgrimage to Haifa, Israel where the Bahá'í World Center is located.

In 1993, Patricia was elected to the National Spiritual Assembly (NSA) of the Bahá'ís of the United States. She was very surprised to be elected to this institution, as she felt she was such a young Bahá'í and didn't know enough to be able to serve well. However, her Bahá'í friends encouraged and supported her during her service. She continued to be reelected to the NSA thru 2001, when she was elected vice-chair.

The election for the National Spiritual Assembly takes place at the Bahá'í National Convention, which is held in the Chicago area. Bahá'í elections are held using secret ballots, and the delegates come together in the spring from all over the United States. These delegates are elected at Unit Conventions that are usually held in the fall. After lots of prayer and quiet contemplation, the delegates at the National Convention cast their votes for the National Spiritual Assembly members. There is no campaigning, and the guidance given to delegates is to "consider without the least trace of passion and prejudice, and irrespective of any material consideration, the names of only those who can best combine the necessary qualities of unquestioned loyalty, of selfless devotion, of a well-trained mind, of recognized ability and mature experience . . ."[108] The NSA oversees the functioning of the Bahá'í community of the United States, and members, by serving on this institution, help shape the direction of the Faith in this country. Many countries have a National Spiritual Assembly, and it is an honor to serve on it.[109]

In 1994 Patricia, as a member of the National Spiritual Assembly, addressed the

Martin Luther King, Jr. Federal Holiday Commission and presented a prayer. This event was televised, and a video clip of the event is available. Patricia also served as the Chair of the American Indian Advisory Committee for this holiday commission.[110]

In 2001, Patricia was given the Indigenous Language Institute's Those Who Make a Difference Award. This institute began in 1997 with the idea of promoting Indigenous languages and honoring those whose service touched the lives of many people.[111]

In 2001, Patricia was featured in *The American Bahá'í Magazine,* in the section titled "Excellence in All Things," when she received the Herb Lingren Strengthening

Families Award, sponsored by the College of Human Resources and Family Sciences of the University of Nebraska.[112]

In 2001, Patricia gave the Seventh Bahá'í Chair for World Peace Annual Lecture at the University of Maryland. She was the keynote speaker of this international conference, which focused on the advancement of women and men in a global civil society. She titled her presentation "Indigenous Women's Perspectives on Unity." She spoke about the significant contributions that Indigenous women have made to bring about the equality of women and men and the oneness of humankind. Unfortunately, a copy of her presentation has yet to be located.[113]

In 2005, Patricia was posthumously inducted into the National Women's Hall of Fame. The word *posthumously* means *after a person has passed away.* The National Women's Hall of Fame was created in 1969, and being inducted into it is an honor. Its mission is to recognize those women, citizens of the United States, whose contributions have provided the greatest value socially, economically, and culturally. In other words, they have improved the lives of many in their country.[114]

In 2014, Patricia was given the National Center for Race Amity Medal of Honor. This organization was established in 2010 and is based in Boston, Massachusetts.[115]

Finally, in 2014, the Google Cultural Institute listed her in their *Showcasing Great Women* feature.[116]

Patricia also found opportunities throughout her life to give lectures, and she taught at the University of California in Los Angeles, Alaska Methodist University (now Alaska Pacific University), San Francisco State University, Denver University, University of Colorado, and the University of Southern Maine. She was well-liked and in demand.

One of Patricia's lectures in particular is worth mentioning. In it, she offered profound insights, placed love at the core of each individual's identity, and helped us remember that all our souls are on a journey. She illustrated what an all-pervasive love can look like for us and how it can change our perception of ourselves. In this lecture, she acknowledged what we all want to become—a warrior for society. And indeed she was a warrior for society! We are fortunate to have a record of this lecture.[117]

Appendix A:
Consultation

As mentioned in chapter 11, the final words Patricia wrote from her hospital bed before she passed away were, "To the Bahá'í Youth of the World: We come to you in loving consultation."

What was Patricia trying to invite the Bahá'í youth of the world to do? Maybe she wanted the youth to learn how to consult so they could improve human communication. Perhaps she believed that the youth could do a better job learning the process of consultation and could become even more effective at it than she had been. Of course, to this day, individual humans often fight with fists and weapons to win arguments, and nations wage wars to resolve international disputes. This habit of resorting to conflict will bring an end to the human race if we choose to continue to resolve differences through force. In politics, sometimes people try to negotiate and compromise with others, which is a good thing. However, even agreements— such as the treaties made with Indigenous people—can be full of all kinds of loop-holes, which can create injustice for many people and can be just as bad as physical fighting.

Clearly, humanity needs to learn to communicate with honesty and truthfulness so that people can have frank and open discussions. People need to bring to the table the personal insights that come from their cultures and who they are. The Bahá'í writings on consultation offer the world a much-needed alternative and a new way to communicate. However, you don't have to accept the Bahá'í Faith to take advantage of learning this effective way of human communication. It can take a lifetime to learn and understand it, but it's well worth the time and effort. Below are some of the writings that Patricia used to study.

Bahá'í Writings on Consultation

The Great Being saith: The heaven of divine wisdom is illumined with the two luminaries of consultation and compassion. Take ye counsel together in all matters, inasmuch as consultation is the lamp of guidance which leadeth the way, and is the bestower of understanding.[118]

Say: No man can attain his true station except through his justice. No power can exist except through unity. No welfare and no well-being can be attained except through consultation.[119]

Consultation bestoweth greater awareness and transmuteth conjecture into certitude. It is a shining light which, in a dark world, leadeth the way and guideth. For everything there is and will continue to be a station of perfection and maturity. The maturity of the gift of understanding is made manifest through consultation.[120]

In this Cause consultation is of vital importance, but spiritual conference and not the mere voicing of personal views is intended. . . . The purpose is to emphasize the statement that consultation must have for its object the investigation of truth. He who expresses an opinion should not voice it as correct and right but set it forth as a contribution to the consensus of opinion, for the light of reality becomes apparent when two opinions coincide. A spark is produced when flint and steel come together. Man should weigh his opinions with the utmost serenity, calmness and composure. Before expressing his own views he should carefully consider the views already advanced by others. If he finds that a previously expressed opinion is more true and worthy, he should accept it immediately and not willfully hold to an opinion of his own. By this excellent method he endeavors to arrive at unity and truth. Opposition and division are deplorable. It is better then to have the opinion of a wise, sagacious man; otherwise, contradiction and altercation, in which varied and divergent views are presented, will make it necessary for a judicial body to render decision upon the question. Even a majority opinion or consensus may be incorrect. A thousand people may hold to one view and be mistaken, whereas one sagacious person may be right. Therefore, true consultation is spiritual conference in the attitude and atmosphere of love. Members must love each other in the spirit of fellowship in order that good results may be forthcoming. Love and fellowship are the foundation.[121]

Remember, Patricia can be your Uŋčí, your grandmother from afar. After all, according to the Lakota way, we are all one family, and the Lakota phrase "Mitákuye

Oyá'siŋ" that you learned in chapter 1 translates as "my relatives everyone." Think of her, study her life, and consider her last request to learn about consultation. Maybe you will come up with a different idea of what she meant when she said to you, "We come to you in loving consultation."

Appendix B:
Lakota and English Words

Conversational Lakota

How is it with you?	Toníktuka ȟe?
Goodbye	Tokša
Thank you	Philámaye
Yes	Haŋ
No	Hiyá
Consultation	Wóakhiye

Counting in Lakota

1	Waŋjží
2	Núŋpa
3	Yámni
4	Tópa

5	Záptaŋ
6	Šákpe
7	Šakówiŋ
8	Šaglóǧaŋ
9	Napčíyuŋka
10	Wikčémna

Online Guide to Pronunciation

The New Lakota Dictionary was compiled by Jan Ullrich and was published by the Lakota Language Consortium in Bloomington, Indiana, in 2008. To learn how to pronounce some of these Lakota words, go to the links below. There you will also learn some new words.

http://www.lakhota.org/ALPHABET/alphabet.htm

https://www.lakotadictionary.org/phpBB3/nldo4.php

Important Lakota Words

English Words	Lakota	Approximate meaning
Becoming a woman	Išnáthi awíčha- lowaŋpi	* Sacred rite for girls becoming women.
Bitterroot	Siŋkphé tha- wóyute	Herb used for a cold and sore throat.
Bravery	Wóohitika	** One of the four main Lakota values.
Child	Wakháŋheža	A sacred being.
Compassionate Woman	Tȟawáčhiŋ Wašté Wiŋ	Name given to Patricia Locke.
Courage	Wóčhaŋteťiŋza	** One of the four main Lakota values.
Creator/ Creations	Wakhaŋ Tȟáŋka	Can refer to either the Great Spirit or to all creation.
Dakota	Dakhóta	Friend or ally, a member of the eastern Sioux tribes.

Gate Keeper	Thiyópa awáŋyaŋke	The one who meets the soul after death, asks its name, and decides if the soul is to proceed on the spirit path or head to oblivion.
Generosity	Wówačhaŋtognaka	** One of the four main Lakota values.
Give away	Wíȟpeya	Ceremony to give things away in honor of someone or an occasion. If honoring a deceased person, it takes place one year after the person's passing.
Grandfather	Thuŋkášila	Biological grandfather, but used to talk about the Creator or Great Spirit.
Grandmother	Uŋčí	Biological grandmother.
Great Spirit	Wakȟaŋ Tȟáŋka	A reference to the Creator, or God.
Indian turnip	Thíŋpsila	Plant that is edible when cooked.

Lakota	Lakȟóta	Friend or ally, a member of the western Sioux tribes.
Making of a relative	Huŋkáyapi	* A ceremony of adoption for someone who has lost a loved one.
My relations	Mitákuye Oyá'siŋ	The concept that everything in this world is related—humans, animals, plants, and minerals.
Pow-wow	Wačhípi	A gathering to dance, sing, socialize, and honor American Indian Culture.
Purification	Inípi	* A ceremony for purification using steam created by heated rocks.
Release of the soul	Wanáǧi yuškápi	* A ceremony one year after a person dies that releases the soul to the spirit world.

Smudging	Azílya	Ritual, taught by the White Buffalo Calf Woman, in which a person uses sage and sweetgrass to invoke purity, sanctity, and holiness.
Sun Dance	Wiwáŋyaŋg wačhípi	* A sacred dance that literally means "They dance gazing at the sun."
Tossing the ball	Tȟápa waŋkáy-eyapi	* A spiritual rite in which whoever catches the ball is responsible for the creatures and environment in that area.
Vision quest	Haŋbléčheyapi	* Ritual for young men to seek guidance for their lives.
White Buffalo Calf Woman	Ptesáŋwiŋ	According to Lakota belief, a Messenger from God for the Lakota people.

* One of the seven rituals brought by the White Buffalo Calf Woman.

** One of the four main Lakota values.

Appendix C:
Indigenous Messengers of God

White Buffalo Calf Woman

The Lakota believe that a Divine Messenger was sent to them in the form of a woman to teach them how to live spiritually and in balance with the Creator. She gave the people the gift of the Pipe, which is a sign of the covenant between the people and the Creator. A *covenant* is a promise that God will always be guiding you but that you must also do your part—that is, follow the Divine teachings brought to you. The White Buffalo Calf Woman visited the Lakota about approximately 900 AD, or roughly eleven hundred twenty-two years ago. Here is one account.[122]

It was a time of famine, so two young Lakota scouts went out in search of food. They encountered a severe and unexpected storm, and as it calmed down, a white buffalo calf came running toward them.

The calf caught the scouts' attention. Should they capture it and use it for food? All of a sudden, the calf turned into a beautiful woman—in fact, she was the most beautiful woman they had ever seen. One young man was very taken by her, had impure thoughts, and wanted her. She told him to come forward. When he did, a black cloud covered them, and when it had cleared, the young scout was nothing but a pile of bones. Upon seeing this, the other scout fell to his knees and prayed for the spirit of his fallen brother.

The White Buffalo Calf Woman spoke to him and told him his brother had become what he had been seeking. Then she told the scout that she was sent by *Thuŋkášila,* the Lakota word for *grandfather.* In this case it meant *the Creator.* She wanted the scout to gather the people so she could speak to them. She talked to them in different groups—children, adults, and elders—in a manner that each group could understand. She then gave the Lakota the sacred Pipe and told them how to use it. She spent four days instructing them on what to do and said that she would return one day. When she was finished teaching the Lakota, she turned back into a white buffalo calf and ran back onto the plains.

Some people interpret the fallen scout as a metaphor. A *metaphor* is a symbol for something else. They say the scout's pile of bones represents the physical and material nature of man, while the living scout represents man's spiritual nature, which attracts people.[123]

There are Youtube presentations of the White Buffalo Calf Woman. Find the one by Chief Arvol Looking Horse, who is the nineteenth generation Keeper of the White Buffalo Calf Woman Sacred Pipe. He was twelve years old when he was chosen for this responsibility. There are other presentations as well.[124]

Patricia's Belief in Indigenous Messengers of God

Along with the White Buffalo Calf Woman, Patricia respected all the teachings of Messengers of God she learned about while working on the American Indian Religious Freedom Act. She felt they were sent by God to specific groups of people, in addition to the Messengers Who founded major religions, including Krishna, Abraham, Moses, Zoroaster, Buddha, Jesus Christ, Muhammad, and now the Báb and Bahá'u'lláh. Patricia believed that most Indian tribes, if not all, had Messengers of God who came to them in one form or another to bring a religion and spiritual guidance to them.

There is no doubt that many different tribes had visionaries and spiritual teachers, and many of the elders of these tribes believe that these figures were Messengers of God. 'Abdu'l-Bahá, the son of Bahá'u'lláh, referred to the influence of God in the Americas when he wrote, "Undoubtedly, in those regions, the Call of God must have been raised in ancient times, . . ."[125]

We can only wonder about the spiritual forces at work in the history of this land, and what the world would have been like if the Indigenous people had been allowed to practice their religions and their cultures, rather than be forced to practice someone else's religion and culture.[126]

Here are a few of the luminaries whom some Indigenous people believe were Messengers of God. The Wilmette Institute offers a class on them. (https://wilmetteinstitute.org/)

Information about the following luminaries can be found at: https://bahaiteachings.org/search/native+messengers+of+god

- Deganawida, the Peacemaker (Haudenosaunee/Iroquois)
- White Buffalo Calf Woman (Lakota)
- Sweet Medicine (Cheyenne)
- Lone Man (Mandan and Hidatsa)
- Breathmaker (Seminole and Miccosukee)
- Quetzalcoatl (Toltec)
- Viracocha (Inca/Quechua)
- Gluskap (Wabanaki)
- Wesakechak (Cree)
- Nanabush (Anishinaabe)

- Talking God (Navajo/Diné)
- White Shell Woman (Navajo/Diné)
- White Painted Woman (Apache)
- Bunjil (Australian Aboriginal)

Timeline for Patricia Locke

1928	Born on January 21, 1928, in Pocatello, Idaho.
1930	Frances, her sister, born on November 3, 1930.
1934	Took a trip, at six years old, with her mother to Chicago for a dance contest.
1935	Presented a demonstration of Lakota culture in dance and storytelling with her parents in Fort Hall, Idaho.
1936	At nearly eight years old, attended residential school in Parker, Arizona.
1939	Moved to Klamath Falls, Oregon and attended middle school.
1942	Moved to Alhambra, California after her father's last BIA assignment in Riverside Indian School in Riverside, California.
1946	Graduated from Alhambra High School.
1946	Attended John Muir College in San Diego, California.

1947	Transferred to the University of California at Los Angeles (UCLA) and was the only American Indian attending.
1951	Graduated from UCLA with a Bachelor of Arts and teaching credentials.
1952	Married Charles "Ned" Locke.
1954	Kevin Locke born in Los Angeles.
1956	Winona Locke born in Los Angeles area.
1959	Moved to Great Falls, Montana.
1961	Moved back to Los Angeles.
1966	Moved to Anchorage.
1967	Opened welcome center in Anchorage and advised Alaska Native leaders on how to advocate for the needs of their communities.
1970	Received Lakota name.
1970	Taught at Alaska Methodist University during the summer.
1970	Moved to Boulder, Colorado to work for Western Interstate Counsel on Higher Education (WICHE).
1972	Helped open six Indian community colleges.
1973	Standing Rock Community College (now Sitting Bull College) opened.
1975	Keynote speaker to the Native American Teacher Training Program.

1977	Elected president of the National Indian Education Association.
1978	Appointed Director of WICHE Planning Resources in Minority Education.
1978	Assisted in passing the HR 11104 Tribally Controlled Community College Assistance Act.
1978	August 11: Assisted with the American Indian Religious Freedom Act Public Law No. 95-341, 92 Stat. 469. It became law.
1979	Appointed co-chairwoman of Department of the Interior Task Force of Indian Education Policy.
1982	Represented the United States in education discussions at the World Assembly of First Nations in Saskatchewan, Canada.
1983	Sold house in Boulder, Colorado and moved to Mobridge, South Dakota.
1987	Began writing a series of forty articles for the *Mobridge Tribune*.
1988–90	Tribe provided land and built house in Wakpala, South Dakota.
1988	American Indian Religious Freedom Act struck down by the Supreme Court.
1988	Was invited by Kevin to the Camino del Sol (Trail of Light) teaching project.

1990	Native American Language Act passed.
1990	April: Became Bahá'í at US National Bahá'í Convention.
1990	Presentation on the Lakota view of the child at the University of Southern Maine.
1991	Received the MacArthur Foundation Fellows Award as tribal rights leader and educator.
1992	Made nine-day pilgrimage to Haifa, Israel.
1993	Selected by the Association on American Indian Affairs, Inc. to be the Coordinator of the Coalition of some sixty-five Indigenous groups for their Amendments to the American Indian Religious Freedom Act (AIRFA).
1993	Elected to the National Spiritual Assembly of Bahá'ís of the United States.
1993	Attended Parliament of Religions conference to deliver the "American Indian Declaration of Vision," a challenge to the Doctrine of Discovery.
1994	Traveled to Haifa, Israel with the National Spiritual Assembly and met Hand of the Cause of God Rúhíyyih Khánum, who seated Patricia by her side as a sign of respect toward Indigenous people.
1994	First amendment HR4155 added to American Indian Religious Freedom Act.

1994	Addressed the Martin Luther King, Jr. Luncheon Celebration.
1995	Traveled to Beijing as Chair of the Indigenous Women's Caucus at the Fourth UN Conference on Women and Justice and was one of the representatives of the National Spiritual Assembly of the Bahá'ís of the United States.
1996	Second Amendment HR4230 added to American Indian Religious Freedom Act. Invited to Washington, DC, to help rewrite the document.
1999	Elected President of Pacific and American Indigenous Language Survival, Inc.
2001	Recipient of the Indigenous Language Institute's *Those Who Make a Difference Award.*
2001	Recipient of the Herb Lingren Strengthening Families Award, from the College of Human Resources and Family Sciences of the University of Nebraska.
2001	Delivered the Seventh Bahá'í Chair for World Peace Annual Lecture at the University of Maryland.
2001	October 20: Passed away in a hospital in Phoenix, Arizona.
2005	Inducted into the National Women's Hall of Fame.

2014   Awarded National Center for Race Amity Medal
        of Honor.
2014   Listed in Google Cultural Institute's *Showcasing
        Great Women.*

To learn more about Patricia Locke, please visit the Patricia Locke Foundation—a Bahá'í inspired, Indigenous-led nonprofit organization that is dedicated to carrying forward her work—at https://patricia-lockefoundation.org.

Notes

1. *The Ogden Standard-Examiner,* November 3, 1935, p. 2, https://www.newspapers.com/.
2. Kolstoe, John E., *Compassionate Woman: The Life and Legacy of Patricia Locke,* p. 13.
3. Ibid., p. 9.
4. Ibid., p. 9.
5. Ibid., p. 31.
6. Ibid., p. 10.
7. Ibid., p. 11.
8. Ibid., p. 31.
9. Ibid., p. 34.
10. Ibid., p. 13.
11. Ibid., p. 13.
12. Ibid., p. 14.
13. Ibid., p. 15.
14. Ibid., p. 15.
15. Ibid., p. 15.
16. Ibid., p. 16.
17. Ibid., p. 16.
18. Ibid., pp. 16, 39.

19. Ibid., p. 16.
20. Ibid., p. 39.
21. Ibid., p. 19.
22. Ibid., pp. 21, 22; Buck, Christopher and Kevin Locke, "Pressing on to Meet the Dawn: Patricia Locke," https://bahaiteachings.org/pressing-meet-dawn-patricia-locke/.
23. Kolstoe, John E., *Compassionate Woman: The Life and Legacy of Patricia Locke*, p. 22.
24. Ibid., p. 40.
25. Ibid., p. 41.
26. Ibid., p. 43.
27. Ibid., p. 45.
28. Ibid., pp. 26, 27.
29. Ibid., p. 46.
30. Ibid., p. 12.
31. Ibid.
32. Ibid., p. 50.
33. Ibid.
34. Ibid., pp. 48, 49.
35. Ibid., pp. 57, 96.
36. Ibid., p. 42.
37. Ibid., p. 95.
38. Ibid., p. 98.
39. Ibid., p. 96.

40. Ibid., p. 100.

41. Ibid., p. 96.

42. "What is the Doctrine of Discovery?" https://doctrineofdiscovery.org/what-is-the-doctrine-of-discovery/.

43. Weatherford, Jack. *Indian Givers: How the Indians of American Transformed the World*, p. 71.

44. Al-Jazeera, "Buried Truths: America's Indigenous Boarding Schools," https://www.youtube.com/watch?v=AY8WVxOAUNQ.

45. Buck, Christopher, "Return of the White buffalo Calf Woman," March 22, 2014, https://bahaiteachings.org/return-of-white-buffalo-calf-woman/; Buck, Christopher and Kevin Locke, "Pressing On to Meet the Dawn: Patricia Locke," August 18, 2019, https://bahaiteachings.org/pressing-meet-dawn-patricia-locke/.

46. American Indian Treaties. https://www.archives.gov/research/native-americans/treaties.

47. Interview with Kevin Locke, June 2021.

48. Kolstoe, John E., *Compassionate Woman: The Life and Legacy of Patricia Locke*, p. 59.

49. "The History of Sitting Bull College," Sitting Bull College Official Website, https://sittingbull.edu/history/.

50. "Sitting Bull," *Encyclopedia Britannica*, https://www.britannica.com/biography/Sitting-Bull.

51. Kolstoe, John E., *Compassionate Woman: The Life and Legacy of Patricia Locke*, p. 62.

52. "Tribal Colleges and Universities," American Indian Higher Education Consortium, http://newweb.aihec.org/tcu-map/.

53. "Native American Directors to Confer," https://www.newspapers.com/clip/1467024/later-bahai-patricia-locke-keynote/.

54. Email correspondence with Diane Cournoyer, Executive Director of National Indian Education Association, August 9, 2021.

55. Locke, Patricia, "A Survey of College and University Programs for American Indians," https://files.eric.ed.gov/fulltext/ED085159.pdf.

56. "Patricia Locke Biography," taken from Wikipedia article on Patricia Locke, https://www.howold.co/person/patricia-locke/biography.

57. Ibid. Please also see "Patricia Locke: A Shining Light," https://mystar95.com/news/patricia-locke-a-shining-light.html, and Oliver, Myrna, "Patricia Locke, 73, Helped 17 Tribes Start Indian Colleges," https://www.latimes.com/archives/la-xpm-2001-nov-03-me-65246-story.html.

58. "Patricia Locke," https://www.sourcewatch.org/index. php?title=Patricia_Locke.

59. Chavers, Dean, and Patricia Locke, "The Effect of Testing on Native Americans," https://files.eric. ed.gov/fulltext/ED336445.pdf.

60. Atkinson, Robert, "Remembering We Are Sacred Beings," https://www.patheos.com/blogs/ spiritualitychannelseries/2016/09/remembering-that-we-are-sacred-beings/.

61. Kolstoe, John E., *Compassionate Woman: The Life and Legacy of Patricia Locke*, p. 27.

62. HR 4230 – American Indian Religious Freedom Act Amendments of 1994, https://www.congress.gov/ bill/103rd-congress/house-bill/4230/text/enr; Public Law 95-341, 95th Congress Joint Resolution, https:// www.govinfo.gov/content/pkg/STATUTE-92/pdf/ STATUTE 92 Pg469.pdf#page-1.

63. Kolstoe, John E., *Compassionate Woman: The Life and Legacy of Patricia Locke*, pp. 76, 77.

64. Ibid., p. 78.

65. Deloria, Jr., Vine, "Sacred Lands and Religious Freedom," http://sacredland.org/wp-content/PDFs/ SacredLandReligiousFreedom.pdf.

66. Oliver, Myrna, "Patricia Locke, 73, Helped 17 Tribes Start Indian Colleges," https://www.latimes.com/ archives/la-xpm-2001-nov-03-me-65246-story.html.

67. Kolstoe, John E., *Compassionate Woman: The Life and Legacy of Patricia Locke,* pp. 81, 82, 83.

68. Ibid., p. 130.

69. Ibid., p. 85.

70. Ibid., pp. 85, 86.

71. Ibid., p. 87.

72. Ibid.

73. Ibid., p. 15.

74. Ibid., p. 91.

75. Interview with Kevin Locke, July, 2021.

76. Kolstoe, John E., *Compassionate Woman: The Life and Legacy of Patricia Locke,* pp. 91–92.

77. Ibid., p. 98.

78. Ibid., p. 92.

79. Ibid., p. 101.

80. Ibid., p. 100.

81. Ibid., p. 101.

82. Interview with Ohíyes'a Locke, June, 2021.

83. Kolstoe, John E., *Compassionate Woman: The Life and Legacy of Patricia Locke,* p. 101.

84. Ibid., p. 101.

85. Ibid., pp. 102, 103.

86. Ibid., pp. 117, 118.

87. Ibid., p. 118.

88. Ibid., p. 120.

89. Ibid., p. 122.

90. Buck, Christopher and Kevin Locke, "Patricia Locke's Dual Belief in White Buffalo Calf Woman and Bahá'u'lláh," https://bahaiteachings.org/patricia-lockes-dual-belief-in-white-buffalo-calf-woman-and-bahaullah/.

91. Kolstoe, John E., *Compassionate Woman: The Life and Legacy of Patricia Locke*, p. 137.

92. Ibid., pp. 135, 136.

93. Ibid., p. 136.

94. Ibid., p. 138.

95. Ibid., pp. 138, 139.

96. Ibid., pp. 141, 142.

97. Ibid., pp. 147, 148.

98. Ibid., p. 155.

99. Ibid., p. 157.

100. Ibid., p. 158.

101. Ibid.

102. Ibid., p. 160.

103. Ibid., pp. 160, 161, 162.

104. Ibid., p. 6.

105. Ibid., p. 165.

106. Ibid., p. 114.

107. Ibid., pp. 168, 169, 170.

108. Shoghi Effendi, in *The Compilation of Compilations*, vol II, p. 42.

109. Kolstoe, John E., *Compassionate Woman: The Life and Legacy of Patricia Locke*, pp. 171, 172.

110. Patricia Locke, "Martin Luther King, Jr. Day Celebration," January 10, 1994. Patricia's presentation and prayer begins at 2:50 minutes. https://www.c-span.org/video/?53814-1/martin-luther-king-jr-day-celebration.

111. Indigenous Language Institute's *Those Who Make a Difference Award*, https://ilinative.org/.

112. Beaston, *American Indians and the Baháʼí Faith: A Compilation of Sacred and Inspirational Writings with News Clips and Stories*, p. 485.

113. Christopher Buck, text message dated February 13, 2022. Both the National Baháʼí Archives and the Baháʼí Chair for World Peace Archives have been searched, but a copy of the presentation cannot be found. Please also see http://www.bahaichair.umd.edu/.

114. Kolstoe, John E., *Compassionate Woman: The Life and Legacy of Patricia Locke*, pp. 171, 172.

115. National Center for Race Amity Medal of Honor, https://raceamity.org/about/.

116. Google Culture Institute Showcase Great Women, https://artsandculture.google.com/exhibit/NQJyZNfVh-V2Jg.

117. Patricia Locke, quoted in Robert Atkinson, "Remembering that We are Sacred Beings," September 25, 2016, https://www.patheos. com/blogs/spiritualitychannelseries/2016/09/ remembering-that-we-are-sacred-beings/.

118. Bahá'u'lláh, *Tablets of Bahá'u'lláh Revealed after the Kitáb-i-Aqdas*, p. 168, https://www.bahai. org/library/authoritative-texts/bahaullah/tablets-bahaullah/5#838594153.

119. Bahá'u'lláh, in *Consultation: A Compilation Prepared by the Research Department of the Universal House of Justice*, no. 2, p. 1. https://www.bahai.org/library/ authoritative-texts/compilations/consultation/.

120. Ibid., p. 1, no. 3, https://www.bahai.org/library/ authoritative-texts/compilations/consultation/.

121. 'Abdu'l-Bahá, *The Promulgation of Universal Peace*, pp. 99–100, https://www.bahai.org/library/authoritative-texts/abdul-baha/promulgation-universal-peace/4#239678985.

122. Kolstoe, John E., *Compassionate Woman: The Life and Legacy of Patricia Locke*, pp. 27, 28.

123. Ibid., p. 29.

124. "Chief Arvol Looking Horse Speaks of the White Buffalo Calf Woman Prophecy," https://youtu.be/ PHqVdZmpRgI.

125. 'Abdu'l-Bahá, "Extract from a Tablet of 'Abdu'l-Bahá," in *Additional Tablets, Extracts, and Talks*, https://www.bahai.org/library/authoritative-texts/abdul-baha/additional-tablets-extracts-talks/169212878/1#341827961. Please also see a letter dated 27 October 1986 written on behalf of the Universal House of Justice to an individual, https://www.bahai.org/library/authoritative-texts/the-universal-house-of-justice/messages/19861027_001/1#322668501.

126. Buck, Christopher, and Kevin Locke, "Why Indigenous Messengers of God Matter," https://bahaiteachings.org/why-the-indigenous-messengers-of-god-matter/.

Bibliography

Works of Bahá'u'lláh
Tablets of Bahá'u'lláh Revealed after the Kitáb-i-Aqdas.
Compiled by the Research Department of the
Universal House of Justice and translated by Habib
Taherzadéh with the assistance of a Committee at
the Bahá'í World Center. Wilmette, Illinois: Bahá'í
Publishing Trust, 1993.

Works of 'Abdu'l-Bahá
The Promulgation of Universal Peace. Wilmette, Illinois:
Bahá'í Publishing Trust, 2007.

Compilations
The Compilation of Compilations: Volume 2. Compiled by
the Research Department of the Universal House
of Justice. Mona Vale: Bahá'í Publications Australia,
1991.

Consultation: A Compilation Prepared by the Research Department of the Universal House of Justice. https://www.bahai.org/library/authoritative-texts/compilations/consultation/.

Other Works

"American Indian Treaties." *Native American Heritage.* https://www.archives.gov/research/native-americans/treaties.

Beaston, Littlebrave. *American Indians and the Bahá'í Faith: A Compilation of Sacred and Inspirational Writings with News Clips and Stories.* 2nd Edition 2018. North Charleston, South Carolina: CreateSpace Independent Publishing Platform, July 13, 2001.

Buck, Christopher. *Bahá'í Faith: The Basics.* New York: Routledge, 2020.

———. "The Return of the White Buffalo Calf Woman." Part 3 of *Indigenous Messengers of God.* March 22, 2014. https://bahaiteachings.org/return-of-white-buffalo-calf-woman/.

Buck, Christopher and Kevin Locke. "Pressing on to Meet the Dawn: Patricia Locke." Part 47 of *Indigenous Messengers of God.* Aug 18, 2019. https://bahaiteachings.org/pressing-meet-dawn-patricia-locke/.

————. "Patricia Locke's Dual Belief in White Buffalo Calf Woman and Bahá'u'lláh," Part 89 of *Indigenous Messengers of God*. January 18, 2022. https://bahaiteachings.org/patricia-lockes-dual-belief-in-white-buffalo-calf-woman-and-bahaullah/.

————. "Why Indigenous Messengers of God Matter." Part 67 of *Indigenous Messengers of God*. July 19, 2020. https://bahaiteachings.org/why-the-indigenous-messengers-of-god-matter/.

Bureau of Indian Affairs. https://www.bia.gov/bia.

"Chief Arvol Looking Horse Speaks of the White Buffalo Calf Woman Prophecy." Posted August 27, 2010. https://youtu.be/PHqVdZmpRgI.

Department of the Interior. https://www.doi.gov/.

Indigenous Language Institute. *Those Who Make a Difference Award*. https://ilinative.org/.

Interviews with Kevin Locke and Ohíyes'a Locke. June–July, 2021.

"Indian Exhibit at School Here." *The Ogden Standard-Examiner*. Ogden, Utah. November 3, 1935. https://www.newspapers.com/clip/1597433/patricia-mcgillis-later-patricia/.

Kolstoe, John E. *Compassionate Woman: The Life and Legacy of Patricia Locke*. Wilmette, Illinois: Bahá'í Publishing Trust, 2011.

Lakota Sounds and Letters. http://www.lakhota.org/
ALPHABET/alphabet.htm.

MacArthur Foundation Fellows. https://www.macfound.
org/ and https://www.macfound.org/fellows/class-
of-1991/patricia-locke.

More or Less Personal. *Lincoln Journal Star.* Lincoln,
Nebraska. February 4, 1970, p. 4. https://www.
newspapers.com/clip/1467047/later-bahai-patricia-
locke-interviewed/.

National Center for Race Amity. "2014 Medal of Honor
Recipient: Patricia Locke." Posted January 16, 2015.
https://www.youtube.com/watch?v=0ULcK1B7IRE.

"Native American Directors to Confer." *The Post-Standard.*
Syracuse, New York. May 2, 1975, p. 36. https://
www.newspapers.com/clip/1467024/later-bahai-
patricia-locke-keynote/.

New Lakota Dictionary Online. https://www.
lakotadictionary.org/phpBB3/nldo4.php.

Oliver, Myrna. "Patricia Locke, 73; Helped 17 Tribes Start
Indian Colleges." *The Los Angeles Times.* November
3, 2001. https://www.latimes.com/archives/la-xpm-
2001-nov-03-me-65246-story.html.

"Patricia Locke." Google Cultural Institute's *Showcasing
Great Women.* https://artsandculture.google.com/asset/
patricia-locke-kevin-locke/bgGVqErjzzNCLQ.

Reneau, Annie. "Shining Lamp: Patricia Locke (1928–2001)." *Brilliant Star Magazine.* April 1, 2020. https://brilliantstarmagazine.org/articles/patricia-locke-1928-20011.

Talley, Radiance. *5 Inspirational Bahá'í Women in American History.* March 31, 2020. https://bahaiteachings.org/inspirational-bahai-women-american-history/.

The Patricia Locke Foundation. https://patricialockefoundation.org/.

Tribal Colleges and Universities. http://newweb.aihec.org/tcu-map/.

Weatherford, Jack. *Indian Givers: How the Indians of American Transformed the World.* New York: Crown Publishers, 1988.

"What is the Doctrine of Discovery?" https://doctrineofdiscovery.org/what-is-the-doctrine-of-discovery/ and https://www.uua.org/racial-justice/dod/what-doctrine-discovery.